Henri Matisse

ACKNOWLEDGEMENTS

Illustrations Rory Kee
Tom Stimpson (pp 8-9)
Design Judith Escreet
Picture research Linda Proud

Picture credits
Cover, p6 Cameraphoto, Venice; pp8, 9,
45 Photo Hélène Adant; p34 (bottom)
Photo Walter Carone, Paris Match; p35
Collection Musées de France; p43
Collezione d'Arte Religiosa Moderna,
Vatican Museums (Photo Scala); p16
Det Danske Kunstindustrimuseum,
Copenhagen; p34 (top) Courtesy of
Detroit Institute of Arts (gift of John S.
Newberry); p25 Ikeda Museum of 20th
Century Art, Itoh, Japan; pp 16-17
Kunstmuseum, Basle (Photo Hans Hinz);
pp22, 23 Mobilier National, on loan to
Musée National d'Arte Moderne; p42
Musée Matisse, Nice; pp20, 21 Musée
National d'Art Moderne, Paris; p28
Museum of Modern Art, New York (gift
of the artist); pp38-39 Museum of
Modern Art, New York (Mrs Bernard F.
Gimbel Fund); pp 36-37 Stedelijk Museum,
Amsterdam; p33 Tate Gallery, London;
pp10, 11, 26, 27, 30 private collections

All works reproduced by
courtesy © S.P.A.D.E.M.

Special thanks to Söeur Paul, Chapelle
Matisse; Maria-Gaetana Matisse; Patrick
Ducournau, Musée Matisse; Jack Cowart,
Saint Louis Art Museum; M. Teriade, Editions
Verve; Victoria and Albert Museum, London
Quotes in translation from *Henri Matisse,
Ecrits et propos sur l'art* ed. Dominique
Fourcade (Hermann, Paris 1972)

First published 1983 by Walker Books Ltd,
17-19 Hanway House, Hanway Place,
London W1P 9DL

© 1983 Walker Books Ltd
Text © 1983 Nelly Munthe

First printed 1983
Printed and bound in Italy by Sagdos SpA

British Library Cataloguing in Publication Data
Munthe, Nelly
Meet Matisse. –(Meet the artist)
1. Matisse, Henri   2. Paper work–French
– Pictorial Works–Juvenile literature
I. Title   II. Series
736'.98 0924   ND553.M37

ISBN 0–7445–0001–X

THE CUT-OUTS

MEET

Matisse

Written by Nelly Munthe

WALKER BOOKS

LONDON

Matisse 'drawing' with scissors

Henri Matisse was a French artist who lived between 1869 and 1954. His life had been dedicated to painting in oils. All his subjects — women, flowers, landscapes, still life compositions — show his fascination with bright colours and their subtle relationships. When he was an old man, ill and confined to his bed or to a wheelchair, he had time at last to think about what he had tried to do through his painting. He wrote: 'My terrible operation has made a philosopher of me...it seems to me now that I am in a second life.' He felt free and detached.

Matisse was weak, his strength diminished — the time had come for him to simplify his way of seeing things and his way of doing things. Instead of taking a pen or a paint brush, he took a pair of scissors.

For Matisse, the cut-outs were the last stage on a road that had taken him his lifetime. This book explores that last part of his life.

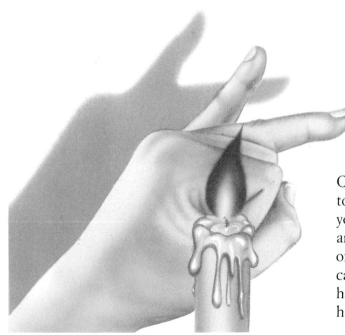

Casting shadows is one way to make cut-outs. Try it yourself, arranging your hand and fingers to cast the shadow of a rabbit, perhaps. You can call this a cut-out because you have cut out the light with a handful of shade.

Of course, cut-outs had been done before. Maybe the first cut-out was made when someone put his hand in front of a candle to cast a shadow against a white wall. And so men began to use this way of seeing things to make pictures or images which would last. They cut out shapes, put them in front of a light, against a screen, made them move, and invented shadow puppets. Later they cut out shapes, glued them to a background and made silhouettes. The Chinese and Japanese made beautiful silhouettes of dragons, birds, butterflies and flowers.

In Europe in the 18th century, it became fashionable to make silhouettes of people, and these were usually in black. This colour was used to create the greatest possible contrast with the white background.

A silhouette is made when you trace the outline of a shadow and then cut it out.

In Indonesia, shadow puppets of parchment are used to tell stories and legends.

Modern Chinese cut-outs like this elaborate mask are glued to walls and windows.

The spreading, cascading cheese plant in Matisse's studio

Matisse's cut-outs are very special. They are not black and white. The shapes he is cutting out are not the shadows of a real object; they do not 'photograph' the object in the sense that the silhouettes and cut-outs do. They are the work of a painter, of an artist. The leaves he is cutting out, for instance, the colours he has chosen, come from a special world—his world. He is not conveying a piece of information to us, but his feeling. Matisse wrote: 'The cut-out is what I have found to be the simplest and most direct way of expressing myself.'

Imagine Matisse in his bright studio in Nice, confined to his wheelchair. His assistants are bustling around him. 'I am like a traveller,' he said. 'My suitcases are packed and I am waiting for the train, but I do not know when it leaves.' Matisse felt that if he was to realise his ideas, with so little time and strength left, he had to find a new way of working. The cut-out technique required less physical strength than the oil paintings of his earlier years.

The preparatory work was left to his assistants. He chose the papers and the colours, and they painted the large sheets with opaque water-colours called gouache. They were then hung up all round the walls to dry.

Now Matisse's work began. What could he see? The light streaming though the large windows, which vibrated over his coloured sheets; a few sculptures that he loved, wall hangings from Morocco, a few tiles and plants. The iridescent shapes of the leaves started to play in his mind. He took his scissors, cut straight into a colour and carved his shape out like a sculptor.

8

Matisse, surrounded by cut-away
shapes carved from his memory

9

Black Leaf on Red Background 1952
size 50cm x 40cm

Matisse, lying in his bed, had a library of images in his head. At 71 he had watched, felt and drawn the objects around him so often that they now *belonged* to him. He was able to represent them with his own signs and shapes. He had his own language of colours and forms. With his experience as a painter he could now communicate his feelings to us — more, he had the tools at last to make us understand what touched him.

Look back at the cheese plant. Look at Matisse's black leaf on this red background. It is not a silhouette or a photograph of the real plant, but the personal expression of a leaf — Matisse's leaf! 'One must study an object for a long time,' he wrote, 'to know what its sign is.'

Matisse made lots of pictures of a single leaf on different-coloured backgrounds. He was observing the transformation of the colours and the individual forms. At last he put aside the cheese plant so that it was no longer in front of his eyes, and let his imagination guide the scissors running through the paper.

'The Sheaf' is a maquette, or final design, which Matisse made for a ceramic mural. Now it was no longer the leaf itself which interested him, but its potential — how it could *work* as an element of a larger composition. These leaves seem to have been cast to the surface like the glittering spray from a waterfall, caught in the seconds before they scatter out to fill the entire page, the whole wall. They illuminate the paper with an explosion of life — like fireworks. Matisse felt that life was like 'a growing sheaf of forces tied, and opening out in all directions.' Perhaps he tried to illustrate that here. You can look at the shapes around you — clouds, shadows, smoke or flames, for example — and invent your own signs.

The Sheaf 1953
size 294cm x 350cm

Painting flat colours

'To work with scissors,' said Matisse, 'is an occupation in which I can lose myself.' Here's an opportunity for you to do so too. You have more strength, more time and vigour than Matisse. First prepare your paper.

You will need thick, smooth cartridge paper, poster paints or gouache, a large, flat paint brush, a jug of clean water, a clean glass jar and sheets of newspaper to work on.

When you paint on paper, you can produce many different effects without mixing colours. The most difficult effect to achieve is a smooth surface. Here are some tricks to help.

Dip the paint brush into the jug of water. Thoroughly wet one sheet of paper with the brush. Let the water soak in.

Squeeze some paint into the jar and add enough water to make a smooth, runny paste. Stir the mixture with your brush until it is like cream. Make sure you have enough paint to cover a whole sheet of paper at once.

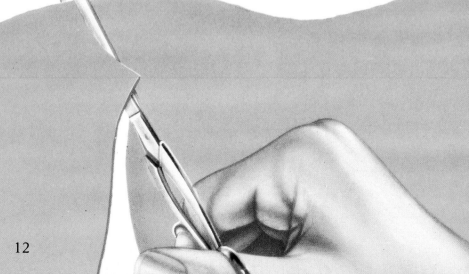

Cutting shapes

Your paper is prepared. Now find a shape. Do as Matisse did: look around you, inside you. Take your scissors. Feel the resistance of the paper under your blades. With practice, your scissors will slide through the colour, and the shape you are hunting will be free!

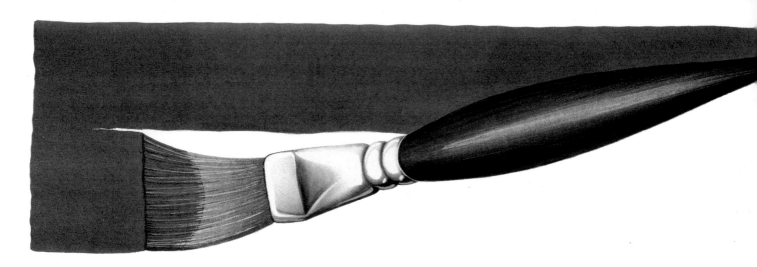

When your brush is soaked with paint, start stroking the colour on to the paper. Using a fast and regular rhythm, stroke always in the same direction, without passing over your previous strokes. Lay this sheet of paper on the news-paper to dry.

Try to vary the 'intensity' of colour. By using more or less water, the colour will be weaker or stronger, but the smooth-ness will remain.

Do you agree with Matisse that a pair of scissors is a marvellous instrument? It teaches you how to draw, to sculpt, in colour. And for every shape you cut there is another! The shape itself is called a positive, and the cut-away is the negative. They are mate elements. Keep both to compose your own pictures.

13

People have surely told you that blue, red, green or yellow suits you. You may think this means that you look prettier or more striking. What really happens is that the colour you are wearing against your skin brings out, or wakes up, the colour of your eyes, your hair or your cheeks. This particular colour creates a harmonious atmosphere that helps you to shine.

Colours play with each other. Some destroy one another, some enhance each other when they are close together. Look at the blue shapes on different-coloured backgrounds and compare them with the different-coloured shapes on blue. Half-shut your eyes and look at each shape in turn. You will see how different in size and intensity they look. Against the light, bright colours, the outlines of the blue shapes become sharper. Against the dark backgrounds, the shapes are blurred. The colour, therefore, influences the aspect of the shape and the intensity of the backgrounds.

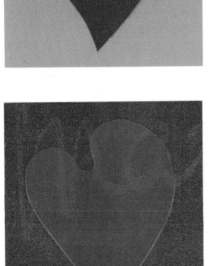

Colours create an impression on your eyes. Stare at each of the coloured shapes in turn, and concentrate. A glow of moving colour and brightness will appear round each one. Now squeeze up your eyes and look at each shape again. The flickering of your eyelids creates a haze and makes the colours merge into each other.

Colours give you different sensations. They can trigger in you a flow of images, of sounds, emotions. Think of blue. You might see a sky, a sea, a cornflower, and feel freshness and lightness. Think of green. You see, perhaps, fresh grass, dark pine forests, peppermint, and your mind drifts to spring. Red suggests flames, and yellow the sun.

Colour can also remind you of smell, taste, an atmosphere around you. You describe colours as warm, cold, tender, acid, and so on, because of all these memories. So colours have become symbols: red for passion, green for hope, blue for peace, black for sorrow, white for purity.

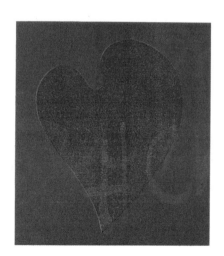

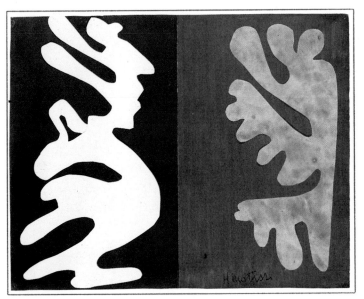

Composition, Violet and Blue 1947
size 40.5cm x 86cm

Composition, the Velvets 1947
size 51.5cm x 217.5cm

Matisse said that everything we see passes through the eye, to be filed in a little room and then amplified by the imagination. In 1947 he was making lots of cut-outs which he filed away, then used as the need arose, pairing and combining his images on rectangular sheets of paper. Both 'Composition, Violet and Blue' and 'Composition, the Velvets' were made at this time.

In the first of the compositions, each sheet contains one dominant image. The shapes belong to the same family, but through the use of colour and texture Matisse creates a completely different sort of feeling in each. The left-hand shape is hard and precise, while the right-hand shape is soft. The left-hand image is put into focus by its dark background. The image on the right-hand sheet is less obvious because of its dappled texture against the soft background colour. Starting from the background colours, work out how Matisse built his effects, and see what they evoke in you.

The coloured panels of 'The Velvets' are organised in a strong vertical format which has a rhythm, like the beats in a bar of music. The complete panel unfolds like a melody. See how the composition is built. Backgrounds first: warm or hot colours in the centre; on the right, cold, lighter colours; on the left, dark colours. If you squeeze up your eyes tightly, the leaves will almost disappear, leaving you with a band of flowing colours. Notice how the whites come to the surface, and how the composition moves, like a long flag tossing in the wind.

Put your hands over 'The Velvets' and discover each panel slowly, one after the other. Move from left to right, from right to left, or from the centre. Open your hands over the large orange panel, then move them apart. Slowly the black shapes appear and block in those warm, glowing effects. If you look at a painting in a museum, you will enjoy it more if you step back and stretch up your hand to block out parts in the same way.

Light and colour

The colours of Matisse's cut-outs are flat and pure. They have come straight from the paint tubes. But these colours, once on paper, are influenced by many factors.

Colours come from light. A rainbow sparkling in the sun carries drops of coloured light. Light changes colours. Take your sheets of smooth, coloured paper and experiment: put them in the dark, in the shade, in the sun, near a lamp or a candle. Your colours will never look the same.

Light falling through colour can also change it. If you put a sheet of tracing paper against the window and paint a stroke of gouache on it, the light coming through will be coloured.

Texture and colour

Texture also influences colour. The same blue looks different on smooth, shiny paper or on rough, absorbent paper. It is the same in nature. The blue sky when you raise your head has a different effect to the sky you see reflected in a lake.

Try playing with texture and colour yourself. Put down flat colour (see pp.12-13) on sheets of smooth paper and vary its appearance by creating different textures. Use the ideas shown here, then look round for other textured materials.

Roll a cork over the colour when it is wet or almost dry. Or try rolling a wet, painted cork over dry white or blue paper.

The simplest way to change the effect of a colour is to paint different grades of paper. Try smooth, shiny paper, rough absorbent paper, or textured paper.

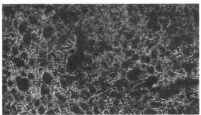

Squeeze up a dry sponge and dab it on the wet paint. Squeeze in different ways, dab it flat, or use a corner. Dab over the paper again when it is dry.

Stroke an old comb through the wet paint. Make straight lines, criss-crossed lines or curves. (Don't press too hard.) Try this using thick paint.

Press a sheet of kitchen roll on wet colour. Or crumple a sheet and dab with that. Or pleat the kitchen roll and press it down. Look at the effects of the folds.

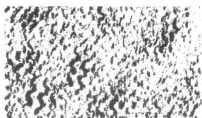

You can make wonderful textures by dipping the sleeve of an old sweater into wet paint and then pressing it firmly on to dry white paper.

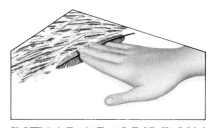

Put a feather into wet paint and press it on to dry white paper. Or lay the feather on the paper and lightly dab over it with a brush full of colour.

Dip an old toothbrush into wet paint then drag it across dry paper. Press it down hard so that the bristles spread. Or dab a dry brush over wet paint.

Oceania, the Sky 1946
size 165cm x 380cm

In 1946, a textile manufacturer named Zika Ascher approached Matisse to commission some mural decorations for his offices in London. He visited Matisse several months later, and was shown the finished 'Oceania' designs. Matisse pinned the white forms directly on to the beige walls of his apartment in Paris. These panels, then printed on fabric, were the artist's first large-scale cut-outs.

'Oceania, the Sky' and 'Oceania, the Sea' are an expression of what Matisse remembered about the journey he made to Tahiti and the South Pacific in 1930. Matisse explained: 'The memories of my voyage to Tahiti have only now returned to me, 15 years later, in the form of obsessive images — corals, birds, jellyfish, sponges...'

Oceania, the Sea c.1946
size 165cm x 380cm

At the time, Matisse took no photographs because he feared that 'those poor images' would stop his impressions from becoming deeper. He felt it was more important to drink things in than to fix them in a second. 'With my eyes wide open, I absorbed everything like a sponge absorbs liquid…' he said. The enchantment of the sky and sea was so strong that he lay soaking in their beauty.

These two panels of only two colours, beige and white, plunge us immediately into a golden atmosphere of sun and sand. Everything is light and free. The white shapes floating softly across the large, open composition, like algae on the surface of a calm sea, provide a new dimension that a photograph could never give us.

Polynesia, the Sky 1946
size 200cm x 314cm

In these two compositions, Matisse structures the ground in a checkerboard of contrasting blues across which he pinned the white cut-outs. The 'signs' are similar to those in 'Oceania' — corals, jellyfish, algae bordering the edges. But here the energy is stronger. Flip the pages to compare the moods of 'Oceania' and 'Polynesia': openness, calm, sand, warmth in one; in the next, energy, movement, freshness, sea and wind. Matisse watched doves flying for so long that their movements glided in his head. The flapping of their wings, their curves, guided his scissors: these white birds could then fly round his cut-out.

Polynesia, the Sea 1946
size 196cm x 314cm

Colours worked on Matisse as forces. 'A certain blue enters my soul, a certain red affects my blood pressure, another colour wakes me up,' he said. 'I don't cut the oranges and the reds like the greens and the blues…'

Matisse saw in colour and light the source of health, happiness and life itself. He would surround the beds of sick friends with his canvasses to cure them. He surrounded himself with his own cut-outs. Matisse claimed throughout his life to be able to control the mood of those who saw his paintings. His friend, the French poet Aragon, always spoke about him as a kind of sorcerer.

Whatever Matisse's cut-outs were to become — rugs, tapestries, murals, religious vestments, scarves, books or pictures — he was confronted with a surface on which something had to happen. Where his colours and signs would express his feelings. He wanted to create an 'art of balance' in a space, 'where everything had its share …everything was expressive…where one had to preserve the beauty of each colour through organisation and construction.' The theme of 'Mimosa' comes from the festival of flowers in Nice, where massive floats drive through hot streets bordered by mimosa trees, where the drifting scent of these tiny yellow flowers fill the air.

Picture a scene of flowers yourself. Shut your eyes and think of violets, irises, daffodils, poppies, tulips. You are composing with a rainbow of petals. Now start again. This time, imagine only yellows — buttercups, daffodils, yellow daisies. Then add a poppy! The subtle harmonies of yellow are suddenly disturbed. The poppy sets the bunch on fire. Add whites, pinks and blues to put the fire out. The balance of colours is changing all the time.

Matisse said: 'An avalanche of colours has no strength. It's only when they are organised that they can express the emotion of an artist.' The choice of colours is never arbitrary. Remember this when you compose pictures.

Mimosa 1949-51
size 148cm x 96.5cm

In 1942 Matisse was asked to do an illustrated album of cut-outs. This book that he first thought of as a 'penny plaything' was to mark a crucial point in the last phase of his career. He called the book *Jazz,* for he often compared the rhythm of cutting paper to the spirit of jazz music.

These three 'Lagoon' pictures are the last images he made for *Jazz.* They share the same title, were made simultaneously and are based on Matisse's memories of the South Pacific.

If you look at these three pictures, you seem to be seeing things in stages. 'Lagoon' I gives an overall impression, a vision from far above, far away. In 'Lagoon' II and III, things seem to be getting closer. It is as if Matisse is first of all catching a feeling. Then, by searching in his mind and emotions, he remembers more precisely and his focus gets sharper.

If you study all three, you will see how Matisse developed such continuity, how he built his effects. The three images share the same shimmering colours. You will find that they also share many cut-outs and cut-aways.

The Lagoon (I) 1944, from *Jazz*
size 42.2cm x 65.5cm

The Lagoon (II) 1944, from *Jazz*
size 40.5cm x 60.5cm

The Lagoon (III) 1944, from *Jazz*
size 42.2cm x 65.5cm

Imagine the intricate cutting involved in making these positive and negative shapes that the 'Lagoon' pictures share. Can you find less complicated shared shapes?

Matisse referred to himself as a juggler — juggling with lines, forms and colours, but also juggling with the visions in his mind. You, too, can learn the discipline of stages: of moving from dreams to ideas to careful realisation.

Your eye makes the link between these cut-outs, remembering the undulating lines and colours. But you have to make a conscious effort to see what fits where and to follow Matisse's process.

Look at the two examples of negative and positive shapes which the pictures share. There are many more. With tracing paper and pencil, follow the outlines in the cut-outs and try to put the shapes together like a puzzle. When you come to compose your own pictures, try to cut out in one stroke so that you can use the cut-away.

Matisse wrote: 'A picture is like a book. Like a book on a shelf…it needs to give up its riches…the action of the reader who must pick it up, open it and shut himself away with it…In the same way, a picture cannot be penetrated unless our attention is especially concentrated on it.'

Icarus 1943
size 40.5cm x 27cm

This cut-out, 'The Fall of Icarus', was also made and printed for *Jazz*. Icarus, according to Greek legend, was given a pair of wax and feather wings. But the boy, being over-ambitious, flew too close to the sun. The wax melted, and Icarus fell to his death in the sea.

Let your eyes slide round the picture. A tiny red dot, much smaller than any other shape or colour, and Icarus's heart is beating for you. The yellow stars flicker, and that big clumsy body lifts and soars. Everything has its place. Whether the stars look like stars or shells crashing though the heavens, is unimportant. The heart is too round, the legs are too short. It does not matter. Matisse is offering you *his* falling Icarus.

Of course, it is difficult to imagine the actual size of a picture by looking at a reproduction. Perhaps that is not important because, whatever its size, you instinctively feel that the space it occupies could not be filled in a different way. The picture has perfect balance. You feel that you could throw yourself into this starred night and follow Icarus and his passion.

Matisse took great pains to explain to his students that the apparent simplicity of his work was the result of a lifetime of discipline and effort. Like Icarus, Matisse was a man of passion. He saw his art as a journey to an ideal land, and the world as a platform from which he could take off. His life was a constant search, each picture a stepping stone on a path towards beauty and perfection. At each painting, Matisse burnt his wings. Patiently he would start again in his quest, and each renewed effort would celebrate his search for light and colour. Always for him it was the voyage, the journey of discovery, that mattered.

The Snail 1952
size 69cm x 89cm

You might look at this simple cut-out of a snail, turn it upside down, squeeze up your eyes, and still think that it doesn't look like a snail. Why not a question mark or a flower? Listen to Matisse: 'That paper cut-out, the kind of volute, that you see on the wall up there is a stylised snail. First of all I drew the snail from nature, holding it between two fingers. Drew and drew. I became aware of an unfolding. I formed in my mind a purified sign for a shell. Then I took my scissors.'

Try to follow what Matisse is saying; live his creative process and learn from his experience. Pick up a snail, or a shell on a beach. Draw it from all possible angles, as shown here. Understand how it is built, find the centre, the spiral. Put a flashlight to it and see the transparency of the shell: you can see so many aspects of the same object — texture, colour, construction. When you draw it over and over again as Matisse did, all your vision, all your energy is concentrated on that single object, and for a while it will become your whole world.

Often by fixing one thing, your vision, instead of narrowing, is opening up and embracing many feelings and emotions. Here, in his own way, Matisse moved from the particular — that little snail — to the general — a spiral common to all shells — from a shape to a movement, from close observation of nature to abstraction of an idea. The observation, contemplation and understanding had been a long, thoughtful process. The liberation of the image from the paper, then, took only a few seconds.

Try to see things in this way. Take a leaf, and draw it — first the shape, the general form of it; then forget the shape and look at how it is built, the central stem with veins leading from it. Let your memories come back. See the leaf on a branch, climb down the tree in your mind, take a few steps back, look at the tree: the general shape first, then the tree with no leaves, the hefty trunk, the branches leading from the trunk. Does it remind you of the way a leaf is built? It may be a labyrinth of shapes, or something with vertical and diagonal lines; or it may give you the idea of growth and birth. A single little leaf can take you on a long journey into your own abstract world.

Looking at a shell from the front, from above, or sideways will change your feeling of it. You may even see the shell as if it were huge, like a cave.

Matisse cut out lots of different shapes of all colours and sizes, and organised this vast composition called 'The Snail'. It took an enormous amount of time, calculating and readjusting, with his assistants pinning and moving the shapes around until their master's sense of balance and harmony was satisfied.

Again, you may find this is a very strange snail. Why such a big picture for such a small animal? And why so many colours? Why cut out shapes with such hard corners? At least a snail is vaguely round! There is no solution to all these questions. There doesn't have to be, but there *is* an answer for each of us. Matisse isn't telling us this is what a snail looks like, or this is how *you* must show a snail. He is only giving us yet another image for our minds to enjoy. Someone once told him: 'If I saw a woman like the ones you do in the street, I would run for my life.' He answered: 'I am not painting a woman, I am painting a picture.' The same is true for 'The Snail'.

'The Snail' might suggest the spiral round which the square shapes are built — the unfolding Matisse described when he spoke about doing the smaller picture of 'The Snail'. But Matisse also called this picture 'Chromatic Composition'. This title gives us the idea that his main interest was to organise the colours in a specific way. Notice how the colours are arranged. Each is against a white background, and each touches at least two other colours. The spiral itself is built of warm colours. The title of a picture is there to help you understand what the artist tried to show you, although you can look for other images. You may find an unfolding caterpillar or a spiral of smoke. Try to use the colours and shapes in this composition, arranging your papers in a totally different order, to create your own 'Chromatic Composition'.

The Snail 1952
size 286cm x 287cm

Woman Seated with Arm on Head
1952
size 27cm x 21cm

'One must study an object for a long time,' said Matisse. This composition, 'Blue Nude IV', is yet another example of the artist's painstaking creative process. He worked for a whole year developing this theme of 'Blue Nudes', although these figures refer to his early paintings and sculptures. It took a notebook of 28 drawings for 'Blue Nude IV', and two weeks of cutting and arranging the cut-outs before Matisse was satisfied. Only then, having patiently created the pose for one, did he proceed to do three variations.

At first, Matisse worked with small individual cut-outs. He would pin or glue them to the walls, where they created an atmosphere of colour and light. Soon these floating forms became living landscapes into which the artist could escape. He started drawing on the walls and ceiling from his bed. Using a long bamboo pole with a thick piece of charcoal on the end, Matisse began to create larger and larger compositions.

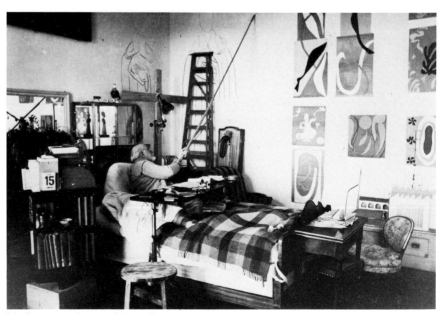

Matisse drawing on his walls

Blue Nude IV 1952
size 102.9cm x 76.8cm

The Parakeet and the Mermaid 1952
size 337cm x 773cm

In 1952 pink and green flowers started growing over Matisse's bedroom walls. 'You see,' he wrote, 'as I am obliged to remain often in bed...I have made a little garden all around me where I can walk.'

In this garden there are familiar signs: leaves, fruit, a bird, a nude figure. 'I had to make this parakeet with coloured paper,' Matisse said. 'Well, I became a parakeet and found myself in the work.'

During the day, Matisse's little garden was growing in his bedroom, and at night another adventure was developing in his dining room. 'I have always loved the sea,' he wrote, 'and now that I can no longer go for a swim I have surrounded myself with it.'

The garden had developed slowly, through trial and error. But Matisse had a clear vision of 'The Swimming Pool' in his head from the beginning. He was impressed once by a lady swimming in an aquarium on the stage of a music hall in Paris. He might have had that in mind when he composed the picture.

His first act was to stretch a large band of heavy white paper round the entire room. The bathers leaping in and out of the long rectangular strip, stretch out like elastic bands. Sometimes the swimmers are blue; sometimes it is the white negative shapes surrounded by colour that give the bathers their form. Matisse's cut-out is unlike any swimming pool you have ever seen. It is unlike any swimming pool Matisse had ever seen. It is the memory of the splashes he was too old to be able to do again.

'The Swimming Pool' is possibly one of Matisse's greatest achievements in the medium of the cut-out. From the detailed, small-scale work he has moved on to attempt one of the most complex of designs. He used the possibilities of the positive and negative shapes to create a whole world of movement, light and energy. But what is perhaps most moving about 'The Swimming Pool' is to think of the burst of life, strength and freedom that this old, crippled man is capable of expressing for us.

The Swimming Pool 1952,
mounted on two panels
size 230cm x 1645cm

Playing with space

After seeing how Matisse proceeded, you may feel the need to wander about in a space of your own. Matisse made several cut-outs for screens. You could start with this idea. If you put small models in front of the screen, all the proportions will change and that background will look like a whole wall.

Before you start, choose the mood you want to create on your screen: calm, movement, joy, anger, cold, warmth, for instance. Then choose your theme: it may be night and day, sky and earth or fire and water.

To make a sturdy screen, you will need strong cardboard. You could use separate sheets or four sides of a box. You will also need a wet sponge and six strips of sticky brown paper tape cut to the same depth as your screen. Then collect your materials for painting (see pp.12-13). To make a picture, you will also need coloured paper, scissors, map pins and glue. 'Day-night' is just one theme you could try.

Sponge the sticky side of the tape, one strip at a time. Put strips lengthwise on one side, widthwise on the other, to hinge the panels of cardboard.

Clear your mind before you come to arrange the screen. First, put all your warm colours — the reds, oranges or yellows — together. Put cold ones together too. Then pin them up one by one on the panels of the screen. Keep moving them about until you are pleased with the result. Then glue each one in turn to the final position.

40

Paint both sides of the panels smoothly (see pp. 12-13). Let this dry. Work in the opposite direction to add a second coat of paint.

Draw a pattern for your shapes or cut them straight from your sheets of coloured paper. You could cut through two or three sheets together if

you need lots of the same shape. Or fold the paper and cut through all the folds for a different effect.

Wall frieze

If you ask your parents first, you could make a picture go right round your room. Look at the room to see how the light falls on the walls. Cut lengths of lining wallpaper and pin it vertically or horizontally, depending on the space you want to use. Then arrange your cut-outs on it and proceed as you did for the screen.

At the end of his life Matisse wrote that his only religion was the love for the work he had to do, his love for creation and true sincerity. From 1948 to 1952 he devoted most of his energy to one single project — the Chapel of the Dominicans at Vence. 'I created this Chapel with the desire only to express myself totally with shape and colour.'

Matisse saw the Chapel as a whole, and created every detail for it: the space, the roof, walls and ceramics, the stained glass windows, the altar, crucifix, candlesticks. For the priests, he designed vestments such as the Rose Chasuble in glowing colours.

Matisse used coloured stained glass and black and white ceramics to balance the black and white habits of the nuns with the brighter colours of the vestments of the priests, 'as if there were four voices singing in the chapel: two in colour, two in black and white.'

Rose Chasuble 1950-52
size 130cm x 200cm

The Tree of Life (nave) 1949
size 515cm x 515cm

The cut-out here is the maquette, or design, for one of the three Chapel windows. Matisse said it was like the musical notation for a symphony: it indicates only the colours, shapes and size, just as written music shows you the notes and how the music is played, but is not yet sound. The symphony only swells to reality when the light has passed through the stained glass.

The light streaming through the windows makes the colours vibrate and come alive. Originally, stained glass windows provided only coloured light, geometrical patterns through which the light played on the walls, on the floors, as in the windows of Chartres or the temples of the East. Later, the windows were used to tell stories of the church or the saints. The windows became more decorative, but the light was lost.

Matisse wanted to return to the original concept 'that the stained glass window is an orchestra of light.' Violins, trumpets, cellos produce different tones. Each note vibrates differently. Suddenly the orchestra begins to play — instruments and notes do not exist any more as such. The melody, the tune, all the emotion and feeling, becomes a whole and takes over. In the same way, each colour in the window is separated, but the light streaming through the colours envelopes us like a symphony. Matisse explained that he could not introduce red into the Chapel. However, the blue, green and yellow glass combine to create a warm glow which may vary from pink to violet. 'I want a church full of gaiety,' Matisse said, 'so that those who come to visit will leave it happy and rested.'

In this Chapel Matisse called on all his knowledge, wisdom and love to express the light he had inside him. Whenever you feel like opening your heart, and then pick up a pencil, a paint brush or scissors, remember Henri Matisse's words: 'One must observe a lot. One has only one life, and one is never finished.'

The interior of the Chapel at Vence showing 'The Tree of Life'
windows in the nave and in the apse

Henri Matisse